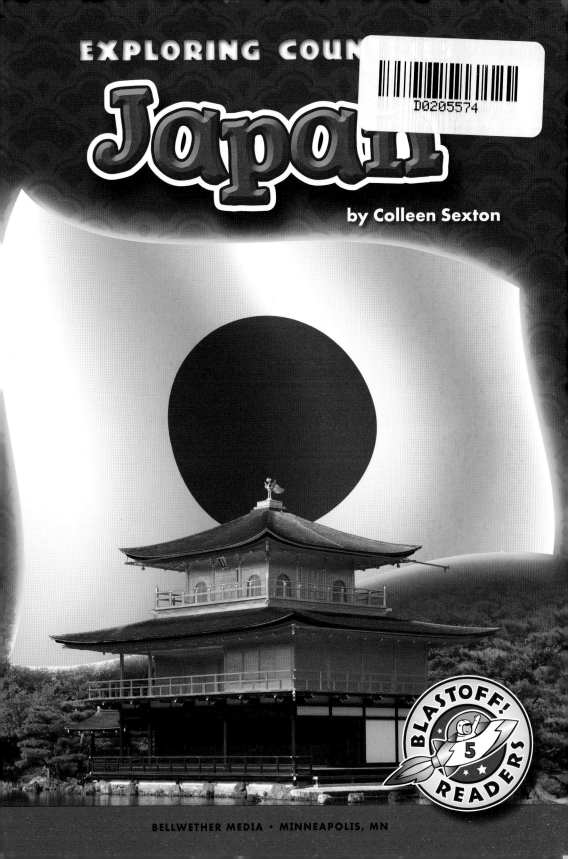

EXPLORING COUN...

Japan

by Colleen Sexton

BELLWETHER MEDIA • MINNEAPOLIS, MN

Note to Librarians, Teachers, and Parents:

Blastoff! Readers are carefully developed by literacy experts and combine standards-based content with developmentally appropriate text.

Level 1 provides the most support through repetition of high-frequency words, light text, predictable sentence patterns, and strong visual support.

Level 2 offers early readers a bit more challenge through varied simple sentences, increased text load, and less repetition of high-frequency words.

Level 3 advances early-fluent readers toward fluency through increased text and concept load, less reliance on visuals, longer sentences, and more literary language.

Level 4 builds reading stamina by providing more text per page, increased use of punctuation, greater variation in sentence patterns, and increasingly challenging vocabulary.

Level 5 encourages children to move from "learning to read" to "reading to learn" by providing even more text, varied writing styles, and less familiar topics.

Whichever book is right for your reader, Blastoff! Readers are the perfect books to build confidence and encourage a love of reading that will last a lifetime!

This edition first published in 2012 by Bellwether Media, Inc.

No part of this publication may be reproduced in whole or in part without written permission of the publisher. For information regarding permission, write to Bellwether Media, Inc., Attention: Permissions Department, 5357 Penn Avenue South, Minneapolis, MN 55419.

Library of Congress Cataloging-in-Publication Data

Sexton, Colleen A., 1967-
Japan / by Colleen Sexton.
   p. cm. – (Exploring countries) (Blastoff! readers)
Includes bibliographical references and index.
Summary: "Developed by literacy experts for students in grades three through seven, this book introduces young readers to the geography and culture of Japan"–Provided by publisher.
ISBN 978-1-60014-674-9 (paperback : alk. paper)
1. Japan–Juvenile literature. 2. Japan–Social life and customs–Juvenile literature. I. Title.
DS806.S438 2010   952–dc22   2010013660

Contents

Where Is Japan?

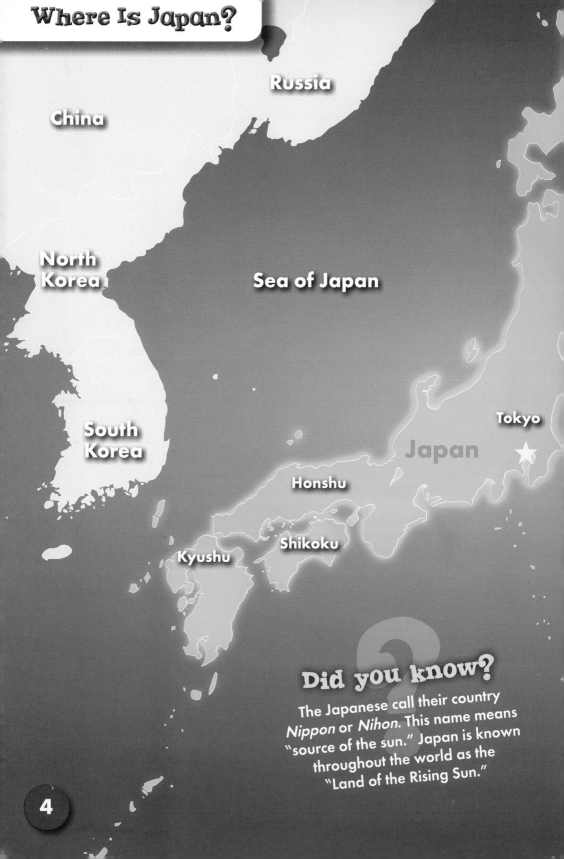

China

Russia

North Korea

Sea of Japan

South Korea

Tokyo

Japan

Honshu

Shikoku

Kyushu

Did you know?

The Japanese call their country *Nippon* or *Nihon.* This name means "source of the sun." Japan is known throughout the world as the "Land of the Rising Sun."

Hokkaido

Pacific Ocean

Japan is a country in eastern Asia made up of thousands of islands. The four largest islands form a long curve. They are Hokkaido, Honshu, Kyushu, and Shikoku. Smaller islands dot the surrounding waters. Altogether, the islands cover an area of 145,914 square miles (377,915 square kilometers). The capital of Japan is Tokyo.

Japan sits between two bodies of water. The Pacific Ocean meets the country's eastern shores. The Sea of Japan lies to the west. Across this sea are Japan's closest neighbors. They include Russia, China, North Korea, and South Korea.

Most of Japan is covered in mountains. They stretch across the middle of the islands. Mountainsides with thick forests slope down to gentle hills and valleys. The land then flattens into plains that spread to the coasts. Most of Japan's cities and farms lie on these plains. Short, fast-moving rivers flow from the mountains to the plains. They provide farmers with water for growing crops. The Japanese enjoy four seasons. Northern Japan has cool summers and cold, snowy winters. The southern part of the country has long, hot summers and mild winters.

fun fact

Mount Fuji rises 12,388 feet (3,776 meters) into the sky. It is Japan's tallest mountain, an active volcano, and a national landmark. About 150,000 people climb Mount Fuji each year!

Did you know?

In late summer and early fall, typhoons swoop into Japan. These storms are like hurricanes. They bring heavy rain and strong, dangerous winds.

! fun fact

The forces that cause Japan's volcanoes and earthquakes also create hot springs. Heated underground water bubbles up to make pools. Many Japanese visit these springs to enjoy a relaxing soak.

Japan lies in an area where the earth's crust cracks and slides. This constant movement creates **volcanoes** and **earthquakes**. About 60 of Japan's 150 volcanoes are active. They puff out steam, smoke, and ash.

Most earthquakes in Japan are small and do not cause much damage. Large earthquakes strike every few years and can cause **landslides** and damage to buildings. An earthquake on the ocean floor is dangerous too. It can cause a powerful wave called a **tsunami**. A tsunami becomes a giant wall of water when it reaches land.

Did you know?

An earthquake happens somewhere in Japan every day. The country experiences up to 1,500 earthquakes each year.

cherry trees

fun fact

The Japanese look forward to spring when cherry trees blossom. They gather for picnics under branches bursting with light pink flowers. The cherry blossom, or *sakura*, is a national symbol of Japan.

Japan is home to many plants and animals. Bears, deer, foxes, and rabbits roam the thick forests. Spruce, beech, and oak trees provide shelter for sparrows, woodpeckers, and other birds.

Iriomote wildcat

crane

Japanese macaque

Japanese macaques bathe in the country's hot springs. These furry, red-faced monkeys are also called snow monkeys because they live in cold areas. Sea otters and seals swim along Japan's coasts. Cranes, swans, storks, and other water birds live near lakes.

Over 126 million people live in Japan. Almost all of them are Japanese. Their **ancestors** came to Japan from other parts of Asia long ago. Then, for many years, Japan's leaders closed the country off from the rest of the world. They did not allow outsiders into the country. Today, people from China, Korea, the Philippines, and Brazil live in Japan. Japanese is the official language of Japan. Many Japanese also speak English, which is often used in the business world.

Speak Japanese!

English	Japanese	How to say it
hello	konnichiwa	koh-nee-chee-wah
good-bye	sayonara	sy-OH-nah-ruh
yes	hai	HI
no	iie	ee-EH
please	onegai shimasu	OH-ne-gy she-mahss
thank you	arigato	ah-ree-gah-toh
friend	tomodachi	toh-moh-dah-chee

fun fact

The Japanese bow when they greet each other. A bow can also mean "thank you" or "I beg your pardon."

A small group of people, called the **Ainu**, is **native** to Japan. Their ancestors are thought to be the first people to live in Japan. Most Ainu live on the island of Hokkaido. They fish and grow food in the same way as their ancestors.

Most Japanese live in large cities such as Tokyo, Osaka, and Nagoya. These cities are very crowded. Workers and shoppers pack the sidewalks. Cars, trucks, and bikes jam the streets. Many people use trains and the subway to get around. People live in high-rise apartment buildings or in small houses in the **suburbs**.

Where People Live in Japan

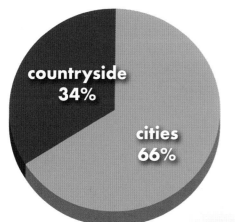

countryside 34%

cities 66%

In the countryside, people live in wooden houses on farms or in small towns. Most homes have at least one room styled in the Japanese **tradition**. Straw mats called *tatami* cover the floor. People sit on cushions and sleep on thick pads called *futons*.

fun fact

Bullet trains are a speedy way to get around Japan. They travel up to 190 miles (306 kilometers) per hour!

fun fact

Cooperation is important in Japan. Students learn to work together in small groups called *han*. Every day, the groups have jobs to do. They clean their classrooms, play games together, and take turns serving each other lunch. The children take turns being the *hancho*, or group leader.

A new school year begins every April in Japan. Students start grade school when they are 6 years old. They study math, science, social studies, and music. They go on field trips, play sports, and learn the basics of cooking and sewing.

Students also learn to read and write *kanji*. These **characters** are part of the Japanese language. After classes, some students go to *juku,* or private schools. There, they study for tests and learn more material. It is important for students to get into a good high school that will prepare them to attend top universities.

Where People Work in Japan

manufacturing 28%

farming 4%

services 68%

The Japanese are known as hard workers. Most have **service jobs**. They work in places like schools, stores, banks, and hospitals. Japan has few **natural resources** to make into products. Instead, companies buy resources from other countries. Factory workers turn them into cars, computers, TVs, and other goods that are shipped around the world.

Japan's fishing crews bring in large catches of eel, mackerel, squid, and tuna. Farmers grow fruits, vegetables, and rice. However, Japan does not have much farmland. It must buy much of its food from other countries.

sumo

fun fact

A type of wrestling called *sumo* is Japan's national sport. It is more than 1,000 years old. In *sumo*, two wrestlers try to push each other out of a ring. They brace themselves with their feet and try not to step out!

The Japanese spend their free time in many different ways. They go to movies and concerts, watch TV, and play video games. Many Japanese practice *judo*, *karate*, and other **martial arts**.

Baseball, soccer, and basketball are popular sports. Winter snow brings out skiers and snowboarders. Japanese families spend vacations swimming and surfing at the beach or hiking and camping in the mountains. They also enjoy visiting other countries. Millions of Japanese travel the world!

Did you know?

Gohan is the Japanese word for "cooked rice." Rice is such an important food in Japan that *gohan* has come to mean "meal."

Japanese food is simple and fresh. Rice and tea are part of nearly every meal. They are served along with salty *miso* soup and a main dish of fish or meat. Vegetables are also part of every meal. *Tempura* is a popular dish. It features seafood and vegetables that are lightly battered and fried. The Japanese also eat *sushi*. Chefs top rice with raw fish and often wrap it in seaweed. The Japanese use **chopsticks** to pick up and eat their food. Kids like noodle dishes, hamburgers, and rice with curry sauce. Japanese families often dine in restaurants where they can taste foods from around the world.

fun fact

Before eating, Japanese people say the word *itadakimasu*. It means "I receive this food." It is a way to thank the person who cooked the meal.

miso soup

sushi

Japanese families gather in January to celebrate the New Year, Japan's biggest holiday. They eat special meals. Some families go to **shrines** or **temples** to pray. Families celebrate their daughters with the Doll's Festival on March 3. During this festival, families display dolls dressed in fancy costumes.

Showa Day on April 29 honors Hirohito. He was the emperor of Japan from 1926 to 1989. On February 11, National Foundation Day marks the founding of the nation of Japan. Children's Day on May 5 celebrates the health and happiness of all Japanese children.

fun fact

The Japanese celebrate summer with fireworks. In July and August, more than 4,000 fireworks shows light up Japan's skies.

kabuki

fun fact

Origami is the art of paper folding. Japanese artists can turn pieces of paper into animals, flowers, and other beautiful shapes.

The arts have been an important part of life in Japan for hundreds of years. People enjoy going to traditional theater. They see puppet plays set to music, called *bunraku*. *Kabuki* features lively actors in colorful costumes and makeup. The actors dance and perform in the same way their ancestors did hundreds of years ago.

Some art forms are part of everyday life in Japan. *Ikebana* is the art of flower arranging. The tea ceremony is a special way of making green tea. People of all ages read comic books called *manga*. Some *manga* artists use computers to turn their stories into a type of cartoon called *anime*. Many of these art forms have been used to spread Japanese culture around the world!

manga

現われる!!

tea ceremony

Fast Facts About Japan

Japan's Flag

Japan's flag is white with a red circle that stands for the sun. The Japanese name for this flag is *Hinomaru*, which means "circle of the sun." Japan has flown this flag since 1854.

Official Name: Japan

Area: 145,914 square miles (377,915 square kilometers); Japan is the 61st largest country in the world.

Capital City:	Tokyo
Important Cities:	Yokohama, Osaka, Nagoya, Sapporo, Kyōto, Kōbe
Population:	126,804,433 (July 2010)
Official Language:	Japanese
National Holiday:	National Foundation Day (February 11)
Religions:	Shinto (83.9%), Buddhism (71.4%), Other (9.8%); total is over 100% because many Japanese are both Shinto and Buddhist.
Major Industries:	fishing, manufacturing, services
Natural Resources:	fish, farmland, wood
Manufactured Products:	cars, trucks, ships, computers, electronics, chemicals, food products
Farm Products:	rice, wheat, sugar beets, apples
Unit of Money:	yen

Glossary

Ainu—a group of people thought to be the first to live in Japan

ancestors—relatives who lived long ago

characters—pictures or symbols that stand for words, parts of words, or word sounds

chopsticks—a pair of short, thin sticks that Japanese people use to eat food

earthquakes—natural disasters where the ground shakes because of the movement of earth deep underground

landslides—natural disasters where earth and rock slide down mountains or steep slopes; earthquakes are one cause of landslides.

martial arts—styles and techniques of fighting and self-defense

native—originally from a place

natural resources—materials in the earth that are taken out and used to make products or fuel

service jobs—jobs that perform tasks for people or businesses

shrines—places where people honor a god, goddess, or other holy being; Japanese who follow the Shinto religion gather at shrines.

suburbs—communities that lie just outside a city

temples—buildings used for worship; Japanese who practice the Buddhist religion gather at temples.

tradition—a story, belief, or way of life that families or groups hand down from one generation to another

tsunami—a powerful wave caused by an underwater earthquake

volcanoes—holes in the earth; when a volcano erupts, hot, melted rock called lava shoots out.

To Learn More

AT THE LIBRARY

Hardyman, Robyn. *Celebrate Japan*. New York, N.Y.: Chelsea Clubhouse, 2009.

Iijima, Geneva Cobb. *The Way We Do It in Japan*. Morton Grove, Ill.: A. Whitman, 2002.

Takabayashi, Mari. *I Live in Tokyo*. Boston, Mass.: Houghton Mifflin, 2001.

ON THE WEB

Learning more about Japan is as easy as 1, 2, 3.

1. Go to www.factsurfer.com.

2. Enter "Japan" into the search box.

3. Click the "Surf" button and you will see a list of related Web sites.

With factsurfer.com, finding more information is just a click away.

Index

The images in this book are reproduced through the courtesy of: Chai Kian Shin, front cover; Maisei Raman, front cover (flag), p. 28; Juan Eppardo, pp. 4-5; Hiroshi Ichikawa, pp. 6-7, 18; Hisashi Mochizuki/Photolibrary, p. 8; Ben Simmons/Photolibrary, p. 9; Hiroshi Sato, pp. 10-11; Juan Martinez, pp. 11 (top), 19 (right), 23 (bottom); Makoto Yokotsuka, p. 11 (top); JinYoung Lee, p. 11 (bottom); Gavin Hellier/Photolibrary, p. 13; David Bell/Photolibrary, p. 14; Thomas Nord, p. 15 (left); MIXA Co. Ltd./Photolibrary, pp. 15 (right), 22; Kirk Treakle/Alamy, pp. 16-17, 17 (small); Tony MCNICOL/Alamy, p. 19 (left); Nic Cleave Photography/Alamy, p. 20; Rich Pilling/Stringer/Getty Images, p. 21; Sharon Kennedy, p. 23 (top); Hideki Yoshihara/Photolibrary, p. 24; JTB Photo/Photolibrary, p. 25; Koichi Kamoshida/Getty Images, p. 26; Christian Kober/Alamy, p. 27; FocusJapan/Alamy, p. 27 (small); Lim Yong Hian, p. 29.